Mike Johnson

Selected Poems

1977- 2022

Edited by Jack Ross

Press

Published by 99% Press, 2023

an imprint of Lasavia Publishing Ltd.

Auckland, New Zealand

www.lasaviapublishing.com

Copyright © Mike Johnson, 2023

Edited by Jack Ross

ISBN: 978-1-991083-00-5

Contents

from Standing Wave (1985)

from Span 23 (1986)

from Treasure Hunt (1996)

from The Vertical Harp: Selected Poems of Li He (2006)

from To Beatrice Where We Crossed The Line (2014)

from Two Lines and a Garden (2017)

from Ladder With No Rungs (2019)

from The Toy Box, book one of Raising Light Trilogy (2020)

from Hide Your Eyes: The Rumi Poems book two of Raising Light Trilogy (2020)

from Extinction Rebellion: A Tribute book three of Raising Light Trilogy (2020)

from Flippity Fluppity Flop (2021)

from Sketches (2022)

Introduction

I want you to think about it, she said
I am, he said

it's not helping, she said

These lines, from Mike Johnson's eighth book of poems, *Ladder without Rungs* (2019), seem to me to provide an excellent point of entry to his poetry to date.

The major themes declared themselves as early as his first book, *The Palanquin Ropes* (1983), and have remained consistent throughout. There's an interest in spareness, in the kind of short, pithy verses we associate with Zen Buddhism or the Sufi poet Rumi. There's also a strong sense of humour, as we can see in this abrupt and yet so-very-believable dialogue between a man and a woman.

The immense complexity of human relationships, social, sexual and everyday is at the heart of much of Mike's best poetry. However, there's an almost equal pull towards the empyrean: the cosmic mysteries of nature and the visible world, the beauty of the birds, trees and beaches which surround him in his longtime home-base, Waiheke Island.

Waiheke seems to act as a kind of analogue to Neruda's Isla Negra for Mike. Its location, off the shores of New Zealand's most populous city, Auckland, and yet its comparative isolation from the pressures of metropolitan life, have combined to make it an admirable microcosm for the type of writing he wants to do.

There's a close social circle of family, neighbours and friends to chronicle – but there are also the follies of the tourists to marvel at – above all, though, there's the sheer physical beauty of the place.

This is brilliantly expressed in the small book of short, three-line verses, *Two Lines and a Garden*, accompanied by drawings by Mike's partner, Leila Lees, which he published in 2017:

> *after everything,*
> *I still want to write love songs*
> *and hear the tides of rain on the aluminium roof*

or, perhaps even more appositely:

> *mountain, beach, and valley, sky and stone*
> *these are conversations of our art*
> *in the garden, snails come and go*

Mike began his writing career as a poet, back in the early 1980s, before the success of his first novel *Lear: The Shakespeare Company Plays Lear at Babylon* in 1986 redefined him in the eyes of the majority of readers as a novelist first and foremost.

That's never been how he sees it, though. Like many New Zealand writers, Mike can switch from one medium to the other with admirable ease. Reading back over the whole sweep of his published poetry, the 13 collections he's published since 1983, any desire we might feel to pigeonhole him as a prose writer who also writes poetry seems impossible to sustain.

As you'll see from the selections included below, Mike began as he meant to go on. There's no excess wordage in a Mike Johnson poem: there is, however, a consolidation of themes and ideas from poem to poem. It's as if the same ideas, about our smallness in face of the universe we inhabit, the need to steward our environment, and the imperative to feel empathy for the downtrodden and beleaguered, must be stated and restated in the hopes that they might, one day, actually be *heard*.

There's no way that a selection such as this can replace the experience of reading his original books in their entirety. Only a collected poems could do that, but even then the physical beauty of so many of the books as artefacts – those illustrated by his partner, artist and writer Leila Lees, in particular – could not really be reproduced.

Those designs and layouts have grown more ambitious and more tactile over the years. The colourful geometric shapes of *To Beatrice Where We Cross The Line* (2014) have morphed into the wonderful flip book absurdities of his 2021 book of nonsense rhymes "for the young at heart," *Flippity Fluppity Flop*, written in collaboration with the inimitable Daniela Gast.

It's hard to argue that this represents a change or new development in his writing, though, when you look back on the strong physicality of such early books as *From a Woman in Mt Eden Prison & Drawing Lessons* (1984) and *Standing Wave* (1985), both printed by Warwick Jordan on his handpress at Hard Echo Press.

Both as a novelist and a poet, Mike has never really formed part of a group or a movement. He's marched to his own drum, followed his own path. If, however, I were to look for analogues for his poetry, I think I'd probably start the search well outside

New Zealand, with a writer such as Ursula K. Le Guin, who shares both his taste for Zen koans *and* his genre fluidity.

> *Only in silence the word,*
> *Only in dark the light,*
> *Only in dying life:*
> *Bright the hawk's flight*
> *On the empty sky.*

These lines, included as a quote at the beginning of her *Earthsea* series, sound rather like Mike's:

> *for the fish, no notion of rain*
> *for the birds, no sharp stars*
> *in the houses, no troubling gods*

Much though I've always loved that short verse of Le Guin's, I'm not sure that I wouldn't give preference to Mike's. I find fascinating his notion of a house without its 'troubling' household gods, whether you define them in terms of the classical *lares et penates* or something closer to home.

There's also something of other Eastward-leaning poets such as Allen Ginsberg, Kenneth Rexroth, and Gary Snyder there, too. And, of course, Pablo Neruda, as I mentioned above. Rather than pursuing the influence game further, though, suffice it to say that in forty years of writing Mike Johnson has built up a formidable corpus of poetry: abstract, intimate, politically *engagée*, environmental, romantic, narrative, humorous – not to mention translations and children's verses.

I despair of doing justice to all these aspects of his work in this selection of 128 poems out of approximately 950. Nevertheless, I feel confident that there should be something here to fit every taste.

More to the point, though, I hope that this book will have the effect of directing readers back to its sources: those original collections – some aesthetic marvels, others more conventional slim volumes of verse – but all of them carefully considered and curated works of art.

Jack Ross, Mairangi Bay, September / December, 2022

The Palanquin Ropes
(1983)

sparrow of ashes

song of a moonlit tree

you might as well forget

about enlightenment

the frog leaps

but does not hit the pool

Whakatane air is filled with jasmine

salmon leap, buck
float past my window

shingle moans, inhospitable beaches
around the Rakaia river mouth

at early dawn the gumbooted fishermen
hauling them in over iron light

pound their heads
with a flat stone

chucked into an old potato sack
in the boot

memory!
not so easily put to rest

I've never had a chipped bowl

or a tattered robe

or the faith to go begging

never needed to thread the stars

on a loom of hope

for a coat of many colours

now appearances are shot to pieces

hang in rags

from scarecrow eyes

how could I ever doubt

my poverty

branch, bare dawn

holocaust of blue

touch of warm wind

sudden tranquillity

at its roots the tree

recalls early spring

delved into religions

final solutions, fasted

chanted, broke bread

died

reborn as spear and musket

one blunder after another

autumn after autumn

leaves pile up at the gate

familiar soils

whisper mid-morning in a cracked

hospital cup yellow and dogeared

the border beast sleeps now

the penitent shuffles forward on bloody soles

nose pressed hard

against the window pane

the poet asks

these dry sticks

are they man or woman?

or the flame they generate

when rubbed together

for years we've asked ourselves

beloved

when will these unnecessary things

fall away

much time spent afraid
many hours
covering midnight tracks
I scarcely know if I am alive
or not

where's the serpent peacock
who can jump the dawn
discerning eye of the beast
shield and taiaha?

it's pretty scary
when this paranoia drops away
but I can walk, breathe
even die

the pale moon shows through
transparent clouds

wind through my hands

seeds of stone

musk of valleys

whisper of dust

few things

flung clear

From a Woman in
Mt Eden Prison &
Drawing Lessons
(1984)

feeling at home

outer walls in bold fortissimo

polyphonic sunsets

can't let go – the inner walls

a wasted green

useless magazines

here and there

the velvet arm of the old settee

wearing thin

here's shame's dawn

an ivory torso on a bed of molten shadow –

I wake to the sound of unseen voices

spread myself

thinly

through a final dream

the sun comes in over the ashtrays

parting the shadows with sly fingers –

Sheila we notice has covered the chairs

with her amber blood –

who's been eating with my spoon,

a voice complains

and Jeanie! See how she wimples her ring

going in to the shower

exercise

a cubist piece of wall fastened to a mirror

the sky and I exchange furtive glances

what do we expect?

cinderella

this make up cannot last
till dawn, painted
precisions on lips and fingernails, delicate hair
around the eyes, a spreading bruise
faces hastily exchanged between corridors
ragged already with shadows
and musk – our careful non-recognition.

God help us
God help us when the colours run
and dawn's livid arms
wrap around the smokey towers of downtown
God help us when the moon returns
from the bones of trees, mirror and stone
reclaim the sliding air
and the chisel sparks foam once more
from sun-sickled kisses
on the waxing tide –
and the sky goes dry and hard

A door slams

God help us

from Drawing Lessons

doing a star[ish

morepork's got a rusty throat
tonight

Jesus is back
on the telephone

a few more
won't
make any difference

my wristwatch tells me
 in deep, clipped
android tones
it's time to relax   axe

fuck that

a long way to go   yet

exercise four

and the voices of the gods
to still, just once

their unceasing tumult

there are plenty of spaces and holes
to let the universe in

a crystal lake has undisturbed space

the line ends in a gale of whiteness

try
an undistracted mo
ment

there!
colour!

Standing Wave
(1985)

from On The Line

street sign – Oneroa, Waiheke Island

no turning

beyond

this point

from Antipoems

a red paper fish
made in Indonesia
hangs from our wall

that's all it does

just
hangs there

from Coming off the Dope

enough

of that derangement of the senses

recommended by Rimbaud in a letter

to Paul Demeny

May 5, 1871

let's not go into all that

we can't plead ignorance

we know the remedy

words don't lie

but walk the stiff border

where night meets the heart

it's no use

let me

let me see

clear

I found the ten thousand lines missing
From Vol. 3 of the Mathnawai of Jalalu'ddin
Rumi.

        They came in a fit and left in a start.

        Now I've lost the whole volume.

J was a captive of wonder. She travelled
in a caravan loaded with gypsy spices;
when she danced she made sculptures in
the air.

   She was in league with a myth. The
myth was in league with her. At the time
most of us were double agents. Slowly
she gathered around her beings of a like
mind. Some could see each other, some
could not. All agreed with her: myth is
the stuff of the world. She would scatter
us far and wide to warn the spirits of plants.

   Take care, she advised us, *we are
coming down fast.*

I'm burying it
under again

not listening clearly enough
to the signals

trying to make a pact
close a deal

head south

wake in the morning
coughing

eyes hurting in the light

from Medlands Beach

no change

li po, tu fu

li ho

no change

you have to be able
to shift your
focus fast

a few casual sounds
someone's laughter
a kiss, open sky

singing the wind
in the stiff, sharp grass

or even the poem
twisting away
sinuous foam

the cream
an inch thick in the can

no special conditions

that's the way the light
always moves

all things come to rest
on the edge

make no mistake
the edge always looks pretty much

the same
no matter which way you come at it

death never was
particle nor wave

foam glides up the sand
just so far

there must be a justice
in these things

the sun shifts its weight on the water

memory rock

sky climbs
the stiff face of a wave

this Medlands, such a perfect
scoop of sand

nothing to mar the line
of the eye

back a simple hundred years
with the ebb

nothing moves this side of the black stump
nor a history

and the beach sweeps steep
chaos and darkness

from the riptide out, and yet
a certain economy of line

in the words

carved into the stone

in memory park:

THE PIONEER MEDLAND FAMILY

LOVED THIS DISTRICT

WHERE THEY FINDING WASTE

PRODUCED WORTH

today the family still ensures

that flowers always bloom in memory park

otherwise

there'd be nothing much here

but a few rocks shaped into steps

a peeling sign

and

a couple of aging pohutukawa trees

Span 23
(September 1986)

the children

the children are dancing

they dance
with the old men

first one step
then the other

the old men are dancing

they dance
with the children

first one step
then the other

the children are laughing

they laugh
with the old men

their eyes are dancing

the old men
catch their breath
in their chests

the children are dancing

Treasure Hunt
(1996)

2

Learning to read is like trying to walk on your hands –
there are signs and symbols from the front door to the road
you must decipher upsidedown
without the benefit of letterboxes
forehead in the clay

learning to read
is learning to search for something – for a Sign, a Clue, a face,
for somebody half remembered or nearly forgotten
in moments when forgetting doesn't work

You walk up into the air in your new light body
as if you were a pair of pyjamas on a windy washing line
with an open sky to play in
but you do not find her there

You scratch in the ground with homely fingers
like a domestic cock on the free range
digging up gifts
but do not find her there

You empty the wardrobe and look under the bed
where sorrows are stacked in suitcases and cartons
and old papers cheerfully neglect their lines
but there's no sign of life

You climb the monkey-puzzle tree and pace the pages of the
streets
only to find things painted and things peeling, you run
to the midnight sea and stir up the blue phosphorescence
with heaving legs and wild shouts
but when you look back the beach is empty

You open the bed and lay your face on the sheets
but their perfume is merely haunting, you rub your body
until it is as polished as the moon
but she does not appear – read on
read on

Friendship you will recognise for its constancy,
grief you will decode from its weight;
words you will love for their sing-song sea-saw,
truth for its touch.
Learning to read is like turning a very metal key;
the first Clue lies
on the other side of the door

4

Here there are signs which don't so much exist
as float; by your own confession they are made over
into something else

which hoards its language close
and loosens its meaning in gasps of things:

an empty bottle with an undressed neck
a burnt surrender on a broken green saucer of Chinese design
a packet of Park Drive that never fills
a morning that starts too early and ends with the moon
in what's said to be Pisces
the cheap sound rain makes on the aluminium roof
food that comes hot out of the ground as it were born there
moths that bear their eyes on the end of stalks
a telephone that drowns in a particular silence
summer that won't let go

In the territory of Clues, everything stands for something else
like an emblem or a heartbeat or a fiction:
the bottle blushes from memory
the broken saucer seeks its unbroken twin and finds comfort there

an empty chair returns to the table, as apologetic as a late guest
the Sword Maiden will finish making her golden belt
and surrender her sword to Autumn
while you
will step on up
into your hesitant bones

5

If the telephone rings, don't answer
there are dangerous voices on the line:

it might be a Debt Collection Agency
a Heavy Breather
the Wrong Number that keeps you talking for hours
an empty bottle of Chardonnay in search of solace
your Dead Father with further requests for blood
an answer phone looking for Compatible Faxes
a Best Friend who's always ringing
just to hang up on you Forever

Not a Sign let alone a Clue let alone a treasure
let alone mercy

Instead go into the soundless room with the telephone that never rings
whose dial has no numbers
whose receiver is always luminous
whose mouthpiece is shaped for gentleness
whose handset is fitted to bear affection
and whose divine voice always keeps repeating
the same message:
please ring back

7

Be glad there's still a morepork or two left
to make the night eerie – standing in the kitchen, hands slick
with soapy water, I look out the window
as one of these shy owls lands on a manuka branch
and stares in at me with her big, brown
unblinking eyes. I ask, 'What are you doing, bird,
out and about before twilight. And you must know
this is the Kingdom of Claws.'

'I am here with a message,'
the bird says, 'I carry an omen on my wings.'
'What is it?' I ask, quickly drying my hands.
'Just this,' says the bird and flies away.

You must find the bird. You must
lower yourself into the disillusioned depths of her prescient eyes,
you must hold her in your hands without claws
        you must lift her sleeping wings
and read in the feathered pattern of moon and cloud
        the riddle of her flight.

10

Look for this one in the most ordinary places.

Under the sink, among the crockery, in the medicine box
in the cupboard with the dead spider
on some shelf that's already humble with dust
jammed down the side of a sofa
or in a matchbox with the Acorn Man.

In a most obvious place already worn down
by the eye
and as domestic as a sultana cake in a child's hand
as straightforward as a pile of unwashed dishes
as familiar as the memory-soaked smell of porridge
and where old leaves make new mulch
there is
a message written in the same hand – the parcel
is always delivered to the right address
someone told you

11

Go to the city if you have the gall
and walk the licentious theatres of Skull
until your knees give out; none of these faces adds up

to a single Face
and the figure you seek is just another stranger
whose eyes will wash over you like an ambulance light
before moving on – you are once more in the House of Tip Top
under the Sign of the Hot Pie, scanning for demons.

Go up to the park where the University Tower rises
out of a child's book and Queen Victoria faces away from the sea
towards the empty band-rotunda, and you will find there
where the paths fork, a park bench
worn smooth by too many anonymous backsides
to mean anything really personal.

You sit in it anyway, if only for the sake of form,
gallop your fingers on the empty space beside you
and eavesdrop on some lost conversation.
'Time doesn't heal, it numbs,' someone says,
so you take off your watch and toss it into red and yellow leaves
its hands pointing in all directions – now the weight is off your wrist
you see the black tower of Skull, dark and ponderous, rise about you,
its lopsided people and angled streets.

Of course you are dissatisfied: too many clues

too many forked beings jaywalking away from you

too many non-aligned hiding places with circular tables

and sun umbrellas advertising beer

too many shadows that take sides whichever side

of the street you walk

not enough crimson in the maple for the venerable sage

who sits up on your shoulder directing traffic –

not enough paper for the chase.

When you reach a familiar downtown taxi-stand and cash-flow machine

and the closed doors of a once familiar bar as the clock strikes nine

in its Cinderella tones and no face returns from the night, you decide

there are only clues here, nothing else; Coopers and Lybrand

circle the sky where the police chopper rides shotgun,

Queen Street tips its freight of buses and people

down to the water and the Gulf Ferries. There are

only clues here, no Clue; only corners, no soft landing place;

and when you finally search your pockets for what you hope to find

you'll see a reminder note you wrote to yourself on the back of a ticket

and you'll know from the sudden roar in your blood

that it has arrived on time

13

There are Clues that can be found
when you are in the grip of a particular feeling
and you'd rather not have to

get up before dawn, look into the harlequin glass
and hear someone say, 'I can't go on like this –
if I go on like this, it will kill me.'

And if your ear knows the voice and the voice comes
from inside this tight wire, then look
to where the first shot of light hits
some unassuming piece of planked flooring in the corner of the mirror
on the dusty eyelids of Skull,

it is there you must prostrate yourself
and put your forehead down – you'll find
your precious Clue
between the tongue and the groove

17

Certain things you will notice, little irrelevancies
that bear no relation to any particular Sign –
how the early morning ant casts
a tall shadow, how the wounded edges of the air
heal slowly as a jet recedes, how the days go on changing
though time has stopped, how nothing moves unless it rhymes with sound
or makes some implicate connection.

These things happen all at once, everywhere, and so thumb their noses
at time and eternity; the day your heart stopped
piwakawaka came fluttering into the house to perch on every
promising ledge and bedpost to call up coffins in a high, pure voice
out of the autumn harvest, and peck at the bread you bake
to feed hungry hands.

19

The chase ends in the dissipation of moons –
there is a Sign you will fall right through
which cannot be sought or found, which
you must invite somehow to find you.

To do this you must make yourself ready with the most tender
vulnerabilities, be like the fresh-baked bread, prepared to let go
Clue and Treasure, to open and be Opened
with the blessing of apples
with the starling sunrise
with honey and porridge
with the laughter of children
as the kereru stands high on his tail, wings stretched
to hold the dimension of air.

Some clues erupt from the smell of coffee the angle
of a cigarette, a phrase or phoneme; or drop on you out of nowhere
if you're sitting in the right place. Sometimes
you have to pick up the telephone and meet a ghost.

Here is a Clue with a quantum heart not to be pinned down
to location and momentum without the sacrifice of one or the other;
it slips from the eye and empties the hand with a sleight of mind

until there's no voice left to say hello

or a proper goodbye –

to get this one you have to pretend to be some Zen Master or

practised in levitation, let's see if it can catch you

in a net of stars

from Open Sonnets

from Intricate Acts

Night of the blue moon a warm northerly rain comes down,
tickling the roof and lightly scribbling on the windows – I wake up

at the beginning of time, dreaming of a child's balloon
and the small, hopeful hand that reaches for it, of fish that flick

in and out of the bloodstream as if they were birds. Before dawn
nothing has been quite invented yet; the air itself craves invention,

the dream still walks around inside my hand
while the window fills up with the world quietly and without fuss.

At this hour we do not quite occupy our bodies, or, if we do
it is in a general way, amorphously, not stopping at the edge of our

skins by spilling over, as a child will fight the lines with colour
in a colouring-in book, into the spaces around us, time also

folded and stretched; and when our arms go round each other there's
no clear sense of who is who, or whose sleep smells so sweet.

They've all gone mad, love. There's Nanu, ringing me up
at 3 am with Druid Conspiracies, and Grace, who turned

her temples into electrodes to shake out love, and April
whose husband turned into a woman and flew away

and Jackie who cuts herself up to make herself whole.
This is it. Life this side of the

black stump, kitchens and spouses who turn like deep-sea divers
on a wreck, reaching for books on reincarnation

and co-dependence, dildos and vibrators with the mouths
of sharks; it's one big party, and it's spring

the moving season, jump and forget, heel and slide
a little of our own selective madness, running about the house

on a Piscean moon, chasing God through the domestic routine
and falling in love every ten minutes.

On the day another Bosnian peace accord collapsed
Sophia had her third birthday, Leila stopped eating cheese

and I hung up on Julie for a month. Winter always does that
to you here on Waiheke, someone told me; it's a

sign that spring is on the way. While I walked around trying
to come to grips with this ache in the pit of my stomach

babies were being thrown into concrete-
mixers in Herzegovina; I had nowhere to go

but into the queasy vertiginous sense of imminent fall,
abandonment and loss, rejection and judgement.

On the way out, up towards spring, I witnessed a peace pact
between my stomach and my heart, cut back

the smoking, and listened to tapes that keep on telling me
that I am creating all this.

Dark rain sweeps the valley at dawn,
there's snow down on the Desert Road;

the tall kanuka swing and shift against the grey
shift of the sky and a few garbled leaves twist

from the ponga fronds. I get up and stomp around
cursing the hole in my right shoe and the scrabbling

starlings in the eaves, holding onto the glossolalia
of sleep as if I were a man with some secret life

in some utterly different place, clinging to my body
with the smell of sheets and skin and the ache of memory.

The door swings between this twilight and the other
on cosmolined hinges, while, note for note, the rattle

of rain on tin and the swift moving air pulls the day to
with the first glass of water for the first child.

Seeing you after the play
standing at the bus stop

under the street lamp
in the shadow of the street lamp

in your black cloak
in your floral dress

in your warm skin,
got me feeling alone

walking away
down Symonds Street

as if it were a huge stage with no exit
watching for a bus coming up

the other way
... not seeing one

The scoop of Palm Beach was dark as we walked
into the chill shadow of the headland. I was still

testing myself out in a new skin of feeling,
hesitant with joy in the open-ended

moonless night, and laughed;
for where we stopped and hugged we left our marks

in the sand, the scuffle of intimacy, for the next tide
to erase in the manner of philosophy, and felt

more blessed than our ordinary lives would credit
and well in flush with love. Returning we noted how

dark and soft the water was, like stroked fur,
how quietly the night lifted the spreading pohutukawa,

how lightly the sky bore its tide of stars and the thin
wandering line of foam.

Watch us
borne past familiar monuments

and duplicitous graves, drawn
by the gravity of the heart

back into ourselves and
our future by those strange attractors of the soul

we find in others, their indifference
and their heat,

with no remedy
but to ride the photon wave through like

some smiling Taoist sage,
skinning the miracle edge of balance,

both falling and disdaining
to fall.

She chops up her fingers on the chopping board
neat

like red peppers or bleeding salami
peeled back to the white of the bone and

fit to garnish the salad of a king, thinking
of her lover who kissed her wrist

where the veins
are tender,

thinking of his fingers playing stitch and thread
with the sensitive skin of her shoulders.

Black lace, she remembers, has that
smell of pink hallways

and the unclotted blood that distends a long, painted fingernail
onto the chopping board.

Winter Solstice

We stood on the road as men do, shuffled
our feet in the cold, talked of love

and the Cosmological Constant. In the distance
the lights of Auckland came and went

on another shore
like the lights of another city;

a ruru dropped out of the trees
to land on the telephone wire,

a dark shape
with only the stars behind.

Out of our words came *them* and *us* and *her*
while we watched the Old Moon, Hecate,

orbit clear of the bulk of the hill; heavy, flattened,
Void-of-Course.

from Sonnets for Gu Cheng

Skull has a resurrection, the kind known
only to the flesh and to plagues; his epiphany

is to act as double agent for the eye, and see darkness
where light could be, extinguish

the hope born of banners while offering nothing in return
but this eclipse. Skull doesn't care, his

vision now lies with death which, he understands,
has been the true faith all along, the real

revolutionary hope. Now he suffers exile
back into himself again, into the egg he once knew himself

to be – there he incubates new lines, lies, opens himself
for the return of the knife and burst blood

mimicking form, memory, full of rage and truth and
righteous hell, back into the world.

When the man with the grey skin comes to your door
it is no use feeling in your pocket for plane tickets;

your few bags, already packed, lie on a bed
stripped down to a wheezy mattress.

The wicker gate still stands, no proof against
the fields beyond, nor their fierce light; no one

has touched it for years, and it has forgotten
the beauty of hinges, the fulcrum, how once

it swung out over the unknown. Your visitor
is not impatient, he has the papers, the stamped forms,

he knows the score; he's seen tears and knives
and with the same impassive mask he's waited while

a thousand like you pick up their lives and put
them down, pick them up, put them down.

from War Zone

We huddle down behind the pews, pressing ourselves
into the grain of the wood, running our fingers across

its practised smoothness as if it were full of secret doors
in the language of chants and lamentations; below the stained-

glass window, which shows the martyrdom of John the Baptist,
a dove full of white flame poised above him, the plaster arm

of the androgynous saint breaks off, making no sound
as it hits the floor. Nearby, close to the shattered hand,

an old woman lies; when she opens her fist a few old coins
fall out and roll away quiet and unhurried into the dust.

We know better than to show ourselves, but one amongst us,
a young woman, breaks the spell and rises, goes to the statue and

replaces its lost arm with her own; she must think it's another
century, another country, and already the doors are splintering.

Untitled

Edicts have been issued, the guards doubled and queues are forming
at the bakeries; from the cistern a woman drew forth a bucket

of throbbing dragonflies while at night I lie awake to the
syncopated slap of leather on stone, your name asleep in my mouth

like dust in the waterjar Pomegranates and figs have vanished
from the markets, old vegetables hang limp from the stalls, and

around the soft-tongued oil lamps the philosophers talk as if talking
were sovereign. In the courtyard, a yellow dog avoids the gaze

of an empty plate, lizards creep up the wall an inch ahead of shadows,
the noon sky swarms with bats, dead thistles lie flat on the slopes

of the mountains, and I see you, stepping form sunken pools
in the fever garden, radiantly wet, your hand outstretched, while

between these walled-in visions mass graves are being dug; when
the rains come soldiers will get drunk and loot the houses of the poor.

from Finale

I want to convey that quality of light that goes frail
and yellow, seemingly lit from within like straw

in a Van Gogh, or the glow of Lebanese hashish.
Flaxen pongas, floating on their own shadow,

coming into the dark like a lotus on a swamp, while,
across the valley the face of the house opposite shows windows

opaque with slanted light and sheened. I've no quarrel with that,
nor the language of it, nor its ultimate surrender,

since there must come a time when the moon is sovereign
and the light a stranger; I'd rather walk out over hard,

dark stones and the hanging memory of shadow than lean against
nature, abhorring the greying substitute for clarity twilight brings

with its promise of darkness and shade, or
reach out my hand and with my monkey thumb *light up*.

Walking up through the section
to Crescent Rd West, hear

the kereru heave
across the slope;

it's a sound that goes on
long after wings have stopped.

See it now cross
the plane of the elliptic,

heading east
through light rain,

neck outstretched.
A white circle

around
its throat

The Vertical Harp:
Selected Poems of Li He
(2006)

from Poet of Protest

singing the blues on Mt Hua

autumn winds patrol the earth desiccating everything in sight –
indigo flowers light the steep slopes
in the snap and chill of twilight

here I am, barely twenty, hopes turned to dust
I'm all sadness and grief, an orchid under a death sentence

clothes ragged feathers, horse a skinny dog –
at the crossroads I smash rocks with my sword
to make the bronze bellow

at the first tavern with its banners flying, I pawn my coat
for a jar of hometown wine

deep inside the jar, I remonstrate with heaven –
no clouds unfold

the pale day turns into a thousand miles
cold as clay, befuddling the eye

the barman counsels me to take care of flesh and spirit
and not let a crowd of snivelling fools

beat me to pulp.

curly beard

not a glistening pearl to be found in once rich He-pu county –
no more lush orange orchards in Henan, cash cows
for the descendants of prudent men –

evidently, the prodigious powers of Earth alone
can never satisfy official avarice

the great looms of Yue had barely begun to turn
to the quick strong arms of the women, the finest silkworms
hardly started their sticky dance
when who should come riding along on his gilded pony
but some official with curly beard and beady eye
bearing a tax notice:
"If not for the magistrate's fury, I certainly wouldn't
be favouring your house with my presence"

Yue's wife bows low to the small-time big-shot;
"The mulberry sprouts are yet but young –
only when the spring blossoms have faded
will the silk wheels spin, and how they will spin then!"

while Yue's wife makes her apologies and promises
her sister-in-law prepares sweet millet

after gorging himself, the official kicks the plates around
and sends his boys in to turn the place over

autumn on its way

this plane tree wind gives my heart a belt
the bravest lose faith sometimes

lamplight weakens, the cold cricket cries
reels in the winter's silk

who's ging to read these painted strips of green bamboo
or hold back moth and silverfish from crunching it all
to a powdery void?

facing desperate thoughts, I straighten my knotted guts –
from the chill rain a fragrant ghost of a dead girl shall appear
to be my solace

in a leaf-strewn courtyard, the unquiet death chant dirges –
a thousand years under the earth and my rancorous blood
will have turned to jade

from Poet of the Palace

incarceration

the moat, blood red, reflects
a palace in spectacular decay

wind-seducing leaves
mirror the gestures of palace-girls

how many spring darlings seen
from behind drawn curtains
hair whitening to dust?

Ten thousand years of pale days
locked away

from Poet of the Occult

high mountain, goddess trails

a spread of green jewels lances the sky –
through the surge of the Milky Way
the creative spirit sprinkles her fragrance

one who sought to lie with her
tasted something metal and acrid in his dream

morning sleet, a windswept hillside
spirals of moss eating into stone

a thousand years, we have not seen
Princess Jade Divine or her like

in bamboo and lilac groves
hoary gibbons wail

find her temple grave, moon-haunted
by the frozen toad and the cassia tree

scarlet petals weep, spiral soundlessly
through soaking mist

from Poet of Nature

cold canyons

white foxes from the netherworld
cry at mountain squalls under the moon

autumn winds scour the sky clean
to a turquoise emptiness

jade mists shimmer on the dark green river
like silver-laced curtains

the Milky Way arches, swells,
flings itself to the far eastern sky

by the river, a dreaming egret
joins migrating geese

silent, elusive ripples wheel by
scarcely visible, scarcely moving

spiral cliffs and sinuous peaks
one great dragon coil

the same bitter bamboo used to make flutes
sighs for the passing stranger

from Poet of War

found arrowhead

1
Charred lacquer spots, bones ash
cinnabar stains

in this icy murk, old blood has etched
green on bronze

proud white feather and gold-leafed shaft
rotted to nothing

just this thin triangle, blunt wedge
ruined wolf fang

2
I scoured the battle plain, driving two nags
through stony fields, to the base of scrubby ridges
far east of my station

eternal winds, brief daylight, truant stars
banners of cloud, saturated black, were hoisted into the void

right and left ghouls, the starveling dead
shrieked hunger for their funeral rites

I tipped the last curds from my flask in libation
charred some cuts of lamb over a bit of fire

insect sounds died, geese moaned sickly,
swamp reeds were drenched in red

whirlwinds, blasting emerald foxfire
saw me on my way

3
always seeking old things, face screwed up with tears
I scored this severed barb on a battlefield

crooked point crimson splintered
once shafted human flesh

later, on South Street, some sharp kid
tries to trade it for the simple votive baskets
the pious weave to pay homage to fallen warriors

on the frontier

the clamour of barbarian horns lures the north wind
moon-driven desert sand clangs silver as water

the sky devours the road to the emerald ocean
along the Wall endless metal miles

white dew drifts, banners drip
frozen bronze sounds the night watch

come moonlight, the armour of the approaching barbarian army
meshes like the scales of a snake –
their snickering horses denude the green of a sacred grave

in autumn calm, see the Pleiades on fire –
across far sands the scrubby bush hides terror

north of the enemy camp is surely sky's end –
beyond the frontier, the yellow river rumbles
and roars

To Beatrice Where We Cross The Line

(2014)

Soft Toy Goddess

She's called Bella Jane
and she lies about the house
in wanton postures
pondering neglected corners
and the awful stillness of dust

at night she rides the rooms
on long spidery legs
with breathing and feathers
one button eye

hanging from a thread

Eyeglass in Gaza

the camera will ferret out that telling detail
and linger there, lapping up the mind

the tree bends to the weight of the wind
the wind follows the bend of the sky

the little girl kneels to pick up a shiny thing
which turns into a frag bomb which explodes

and takes her apart bit by flying bit, holes in the world,
holes in the flesh, holes in the air, holes in the body and blood

with ice-cream petaled pink or gun-metal grey, the camera
will linger on telling detail, an empty shoe, perhaps

the scribble of shrapnel on the wall, while the tree
bends to the weight of the wind and the camera

shifts focus: gives us a wide-shot, the wind
following the bend of the sky

After Alamu Prabhu

When they see breasts coming
they call it a woman

when they see baggage swinging
they call it a man

when they see the sky running
they call it naked

when they see a dead child
they call it justice

My Father Was A Shoulder

my father was a shoulder

bent

to the wheels the gods spin

around every time they dream – there was milk in the cup

and the taste of sunshine upon the tongue of morning

but in the end it killed him

my mother

made lots of paper children out of the discarded wings

she collected in the yard while she was waiting

for the heat to fade or

the floods to come

or a life to come by drawn by a peacock carriage

or some word

from my father

but in the end it killed her

my father

his face mutilated by work

his shoulder turned to granite

his hands to greywacke

a mere

scoop of clay, filled

with the milk of the early star while the shadows are still cool

filled the cup, rang the till

with assiduous movements magic enough

to warm the hunger which swells

like a bean seed with all its rage and glory

after the rain

then

he held me upside down, to give me

the feel of it

the inverted

bowl of the sky

across which sparrows skip like flung stones

held me there, till I got used to it, seeing the world that way

Two Lines and a Garden
(2017)

from Part One

after everything,

I still want to write love songs

and hear the tides of rain on the aluminium roof

•

if it weren't for your eyes, I couldn't see

if it weren't for your lips, I couldn't talk

without your grace, I couldn't take a breath

•

this is marmite on toast, this is a boiled egg

this is the aroma of fresh coffee

and this is a fresh span of sunlight

•

dawn, and the road is darker than the sky

I can walk my way by the feel of it

looking up at the stars as I go

•

I love to seek out fast running streams

stare at the passing parade

sit and think of nothing

from Part Two

for the fish, no notion of rain

for the birds, no sharp stars

in the houses, no troubling gods

•

it was a quick death and a painless one, they said

I don't know about that

words are easy

from Part Three

mountain, beach, and valley, sky and stone

these are conversations of our art

in the garden, snails come and go

Ladder with No Rungs
(2019)

from the first rung

distance is measured in the body

we approach memory

like beggars

not asking for too far

•

where there's a whim

there's a way

will goes by many names

loneliness in search of a forest

•

camp and decanter

cup and sword

the desert goes on for miles

from the second rung

she drew a line through her memory
there was the black with white shading
the past in negative

•

cut around the shape
push it through

the paper girls join hands

•

rats scratch in the walls
there's always something

there's always the fantasy

from the third rung

tyres crunch on gravel
the world repairs to flame

wine sits on the lip of the glass

•

she dropped a pearl into her cup
it became an ocean

she was the ocean

from the fourth rung

words, can't be located
language is never at rest

a shadow writes in rain

•

I want you to think about it, she said
I am, he said

it's not helping, she said

from the ladder

between the uprights and the
crosspiece
stars flow

ghosts thread in and out

•

the ladder without rungs
is no ladder

rather a flock of birds

The Toy Box.
Raising Light Trilogy, 1
(2020)

from Part One: into the toy box

a house with no windows

they made a house out of bricks and sand
and sticky stuff
but forgot to put in the windows

the man in the moon was sad
because he had no nice glass to shine through

so he went to ask the jade rabbit
who'd been digging holes in the moon
for all eternity (it's easy to see them!)
to ask for advice

you can't ask me, the rabbit said, because
I dig burrows and burrows don't have
windows, silly – deep underground there is a burrow heaven
and it has no windows

so the man in the moon visited the woodcutter
who worked alone in the dark, cutting down
an acacia tree, which healed itself
after every blow of his silver axe

you can't ask me, the woodcutter said
I have no time, I'm too busy to look around
and can only see your light
in the blade of my axe

so the man in the moon went to the goddess who lives
in the mountains of the moon
in a splendid palace of ice

you can't ask me, she said, I've been
banished from the earth forever
because I stole my king's elixir
and so a house without windows
is just like my heart, all closed off
and shut away

this made the man in the moon even sadder:
he couldn't shine in the rabbit's burrow
he could only shine on the woodcutter's blade
he couldn't shine in the goddess's heart
he couldn't even shine on the foolish toys
who forgot to put windows in their houses
of bricks and sand and sticky stuff

but there was love in his heart, even for the poor

chipped and broken toys with their eyes rubbed out

and their houses with no windows, no doors even,

and so he turned his sad face away, to the other side, the dark

side

where the stars alone could see his tears

and his bright and happy face might always

be looking our way

Scheherazade: a still life

the picture shows
a young woman on an embroidered cushion
sitting in front of her king

she looks very composed

the king lounges back, one knee up
an arm resting loosely upon it
the other hand holding a hookah
from which there arise spirals and
curlicues and fairy rings

in the background attendants hover

by his side a scimitar
with a curved moon blade
and an ornate guard
lies negligently
on the folds of his royal gown

the king looks very composed
the hookah looks very dignified
the spirals and curlicues and fairy rings
are fantastical

the attendants are suitably awed

and the scimitar looks as if it were dreaming
perhaps of a red satin cushion
in a palace of peace
with the burbling call of doves
and the quiver of water in cool stone pools
where rainbow coloured fish flick
from instant to instant

she is leaning forwards, one hand raised flat
palm up
as if she were offering him a delicacy
on a plate, her head tilted up a little
her mouth open

words! I know she needs words
I would love to help her with some
words love to be needed
or they go brown and die like fallen leaves

but it's more than words she needs
it's a special magic, a story magic
as each word awaits the next
most breathlessly
and events can hardly keep pace
with themselves

meanwhile the king keeps smoking his hookah
with spirals and curlicues and fairy rings

the attendants hover expectantly

and the scimitar keeps dreaming
of vanquished foes,
of an exalted future in the Hand of God
as the greatest sword of all time
with the sharpest blade of all time
the sword of swords

a proud blade that would never
stoop to beheading a girl like this
this particular girl, in fact
who speaks so sweetly, whose only crime
is innocence
and to have to feel once more
sticky human blood along the blade

the picture shows
a scene of opulent tranquillity
but everybody knows
even the gloating attendants

where the story must end

Noddy - a short story

not fair to say that Noddy is the dumbarse of Toy Town

although his bell does a fair amount of jingling

on top of his spring-loaded head

to little effect

and he is a tad too easily frightened

Big Ears too has come under a lot of flack

for being a hearty know-nothing

with an overfondness for platitudes

and a suspicious attachment

to the little wooden toy with the dunce's hat

the painted smile

and the helpless noddy-nod-nod of his little head

those toy-town gossips will never understand

the nature of bromance

in fact, everybody takes care of the little

nodding man – he never comes to any harm –

and Mr Plod, a cop of immeasurable slowness
of speech, always remembers what Noddy's house
looks like even when Noddy himself
has forgotten

once he went to Big Ears' house thinking
that he was Big Ears
they had a lot of muddly sorting out to do
after which they sat down for a nice cup of tea

not the squarest block in the box, but getting there
and look, he has his own little yellow car with the
blue fenders, he's coming along just fine
is Noddy
thank you very much
and never forget that, like you and me
and everybody else in the box,
he too was made by old man Carver

Goldilocks the refugee

she was little and sad and lost
had no home under the sun
and she'd come a long way
over some hard roads

perhaps she'd been cursed by a wicked fairy
or born to war and strife
in some place where it got too hot
and the rivers ran dry

there was dust on her dress,
her ankles were sore
and when a door opened up in a world
with the light too bright
she had no choice but to step through
into the cool interior
the shady spaces
of somebody else's home

the interloper

knowing

if she kept trying, there was a place

just for her, a world that fitted her

a place to eat and sleep

and dream, not of dog-faced soldiers

or burnt meadows

but a little house, in a wood

near a green, by rushing water

with a kindly teddy bear

watching over her sleep

where it goes, nobody knows

time's not the same in the toy box

it's more like playdough

or that gooey stuff you throw at walls

and it sticks ... for a while

it can get a bit spooky

at night in the toy box

with nothing to comfort you

but the muddledy dreams of Raggedy Ann

in which time does a loop-de-loop

and comes back as the enemy

the steady march of the clock-tick

meanwhile some of the smarter toys

like Jiminy Cricket

have begun to suspect

that they are losing pieces of time

as surely as they are losing their stuffing

or the colour

off their once shiny paint jobs

but where time flows, nobody knows

and nobody knows how far it goes

or where it stops

time flakes off, the cricket said

and Pooh Bear agrees – he's seen

some pretty flaky time in his time

'not every pot of honey is equal in weight'

he says

which is really wise

for a bear of very little brain

Bob the Builder and the Bobsy Twins

wake up in a place where no time passes

everything hangs suspended

the clock stops, never to go again

the arrow at the bottom of the box

is frozen in mid-air, no nearer, no further away

from the target

which is nothing more than a face

in the hallows of memory

it's true, time is not the same in the toy box

it's gone all corkscrew

and put the toys into a coma

you'll know what's happened if you stare hard enough

into their blank faces

and listen for their absent whispers

in the world of lost words

you can't say we didn't get fair warning

when the lights are switched off
a glow still filters under the door
just enough to show something
but not enough to show anything

there's only so far you can go
to keep your promises
keep your head above water
show enough but not too much
just enough but not too little

there's only so far you can go
to keep your end of the bargain
to hold it in your heart
to keep it dear to you, like a shrine
to keep it out of the shadows
to keep it where you can see it
to know its partial revelation
like the time in the garden with
the sunwine
and the starwine
and the crispy crisps

you can't say we didn't get fair warning

when the light is switched off

what filters under the door is barely enough

to shape the body, desire, hope,

all that Mr Moonlight might bring

on the tripwires of memory

and no matter how far you go

it can never be far enough

from intruders who lurk

beyond the doorway

waiting for you

you who are standing by the toy box

in the half world

waiting

from Part Two: out of the toy box

the map is not the territory

the island is limned in black
a shadow image, a history

at first sight, you can't tell what it is
an ink splotch or a rocky dragon
hard to see it as a place where people live
and children play
and the world can seem close
or very far away

I love those old celluloid photos
the tight rolls of negatives
which would unwind
a world full of ghosts
with holes for eyes and bright silver hair

who might or might not have been family

we have these things

we have a beach a sky and garden

a dolls' house

a pretty, vacant space

all anybody could ask

sky-latched, tide-patched, earth-matched

memories patched, most not worth the time

spent making them in the first place

I might just as well have

stayed at home, sailed the winds on a lily

read a book in the panther hours

or whiled away my time in the toy box

between here and let's pretend

with my friends

and pat-a-cake some happy words

pat-a-cake pat-a-cake …

sometimes all anybody could ask

is not enough

I don't complain, I say to people,

but that's a lie – I complain all the time

about this and that and the great injustice of things

the beach salts over, the sky cracks open

the garden floods, the doll's house

gets stolen, the pretty space

crashes

somebody takes a poke at somebody

who passes it on

the toy box fills up with good wishes

as the purse empties

this has to be about as good as it gets

cowboy capers
(for David Gemmell)

sorcerous swords and six-guns –
the lone gunman sets out
across the vanishing plain

where a woman, her two children
and their covered wagon drawn by oxen
are winding their way to Paradise
which always comes with a clear stream
rich soils
healthy children and a good man

it's a big country

presently, a gate to another world
will open between some standing stones
and demons will pour forth
demons that look like men, demons that
look like beasts, demons
that just look like demons
and they make short work of heroes

will the lone gunman be in time to save
the woman, and her children, and so earn
her eternal gratitude among
the piles of wasted ghouls
or will he be too late and find them
their bodies ripped and torn apart
by a hatred too vast for the human heart?

for her part, the woman's already had one man
die on her
she can't afford a second
wandering the Void in search of lost love
and, besides, grief lies like some special curse
on the Deathwalker, Demonslayer
not for one moment can he still
the crying of his heart

not the kind of man you settle down with

the lone gunman arrives at the mountains
the tracks are clear, they head west
into the sunset – knows a rare, quiet moment
with just himself and his grief under the stars

before all hell breaks loose

memories of an arrow

as the night fades
and the night is lush
nine suns appear
in the early world
competing for the sky

a multiple dawn
around a single horizon
nine eyes opening

a great fear comes
upon the earth
upon those who live
and those who scheme

when these nine suns
meet in the middle
of the air
what a falling out
there will be

our hero steps forward
with his mighty bow
and his golden arrows
and his gleaming hair
and his naked chest
glistening

sky and earth hang
in balance

the bow is drawn
the arrow fitted

the heart steady
the eye in line
muscles matched

those who live
and those who dream
hold their breath

and as the gods look
the other way
the first arrow flies

Hide Your Eyes: The Rumi Poems.

Raising Light Trilogy, 2

(2020)

that greater frenzy

it's a pretty mess
what to say and do
and how we make up for it all
when the word gets about
and the girls gather
to admire your dress

from the face in the sky
you can't hide your eyes
or keep your quiet
when sharp-toothed demons
run riot
and Rumi gets left
to write on the wall
after the party
and everybody who's anybody
has gone home
with what's left of their lives

perhaps She could never stand

to have her bodice ripped

by eager slaves

that we might behold

all that is in bold and

open form

lest we die of awe

with no one to pour

a little wine on our graves

for surely

we would die from that greater frenzy

before getting the chance

to clear away the tears

close the accounts

say goodbye to friends and fears

make a final stand

prepare ourselves for obliteration

covering the eyes of our children

with our naked hands

see-saw

did you see what you thought

you saw

or was the see-saw purely

for the playground

where children scream

and throw their hands into the air

and the Beloved walks the street unseen

and unrecognised

secret lover of her heart disguised

I saw what I thought I saw

because I couldn't see anything else

ever

what I thought I saw is all I see

for all eternity

and the poet was just so right

when he said that one thought

can fill immensity

what I thought I saw, I saw

and can't unsee

no matter how hard I try

or what's at stake

or how the heart

might hide the world

from the naked sky

or the naked sky might

hide the heart

from the world

it works whichever way you say it

all in hiding

from that invisible worm

that flies the night

and heedlessly buries itself

in the heart of the rose

most gentle revenge

good friends and comrades

be gentle

with those who hurt you

for they hurt worse

their wound

is double yours

and besides

it's always ten times worse

to be forgiven

than to be accused

so you have the satisfaction

of knowing

that your gentle solicitation

cuts

far deeper

than any knife

cultivation

allow time for it

give it space, room to grow

to show its face

to come clean, to make amends

put on a show

declare its intentions

colour its petals pink

things do not come forward

of their own accord

but need a little coaxing

a little stroking under the chin

a few sweet nothings

for the shy one, the shyest of all

the veiled one

the whispered one

who parts her flesh

only to the red dawn and no other

until tomorrow

this gift of flowers

try
a little humming at the back of the throat
a light drumming of fingers on stretched skin
a thrumming on the kettledrum
an up-tempo two-step
a platter of memories and a book of hours

allow time for it
to arrive, to be

give it a place and
space
a touch of grace
and there it is

quivering and uncertain
but alive
oh yes, alive

the Beloved rules

I went to the Beloved
full of excuses
and met you there

it was an awkward moment
excuses all around

I had to laugh
the look on your face
your voodoo walk
the sudden terror of the blood

a great unexpectedness
opened up like a water lily
with you the dragonfly
wings iridescent
hovering over the still water

we exchanged politenesses
as many as were needed
then kissed like crazy
because that was the only thing
left to do

you can't script these things
you can't imagine them
you can't believe them
but in the land of the Beloved
the Beloved rules
her face everywhere
on every billboard and bleacher
screen and scene

we knew why we were there
and who was to blame
and where judgement might fall
but what the hell
by the time the kissing was done
and we were getting naked
we ran right out of excuses
though we had plenty to spare

and rose from the dead
feeling the wind in our hair
the blood in our veins
the bubble of words on our lips

and the hand we were
each to each
holding

the gardenia

in the inner chambers
with the sound of water slipping
over mossy stones
you remove her veil

it's made of starlight and lace
edged in snowflake
and myth
with a touch of yellow
at the centre for secret love

this is the moment
this is what you came here for
what has had you on edge
all these years
from the time you first
took the sky into your chest
like a swan you glide over
your disturbing shadow
hiding your eyes away
from petals of deft light
and the sly laughter of girls

whenever you walked into the wild
she was there, a power

so elemental
you didn't know her for what she was
or hear any wedding sounds

when the wild comes into you
a storm on the sky's wing
or in the stillness of green
to rattle your heart
she walks alongside
she opens your past
to show you
its invisible hiding places

how could you not
lead her into the garden
saturated by the scent of gardenias
blinded by their purity
inhale her scent
where the sunlight falls
and the world is quicksilver and dapple

lift her veil of starlight and lace
and see what there is
to be seen

a corolla of elegant white

the wooden spoon

Rumi lays out his breakfast
roasted oats, warmed goat's milk
and a dish of honey

he says a quick prayer or two
in case god snatches it all away
before he can lift a spoon

there have been times when
the spoon has left the bowl full
but landed empty on his lips

god can be that quick

once a thief stole the moon from his sky
leaving his window empty for many nights
and a sack of sorrow in his gut

it took a heap of prayers and invocations
to get it back
but the thief had consumed all
but a thin slice
which

with more prayers
and invocations
grew once more into full size
in Rumi's window
large and tasty looking

as he eats, he savours every mouthful
chew for long enough and it all tastes
like god or tomorrow's grief or joy

he needs all his strength
his humility
he needs his bloodsong
all the magic he can muster
incantations and chants
and age-old prayers

it is said that when he was young
he made birds out of clay
and threw them in the air
where
they turned into real birds
and flew away

but none of that is true
all made up for popular consumption
and to keep his ratings high

the only magic the poet has
lies in his ordinariness
his scuffed slippers, frayed cuffs
his wooden spoon
and the wild beating
of his dervish heart
as he sets out into the day

to meet the Beloved

sensual senses

that smell of cinnamon spice
like the smell of wool burning
rich and oily

the chirp of the nightingale
is like a distant call
from a morning that comes too early

the smell of the earth
and the moist decay of the punga fronds
is like the damp on your thighs

the touch of the cardamon night
on your bare skin
has its own intimacy

the way the flowers taste your tongue
is enough to set the garden alight
with a late sunset

and the sight of all you can't see
comes as a revelation
just on time

cutting up shadows into syllables

Rumi stays at home
making syllables out of the darkness
and, like blowing kisses,
sends them off into the night
into the care of the vagrant winds

he keeps thinking he has
better things to do
but can't think of what
at that moment

everybody is out having fun
dancing and whooping it up
embracing the moonlight
before dawn catches them out

but the lovesick Rumi
is not among them

rather
summoned from the forests of the night
to mutter under his breath
frown at the shadows
and wonder how the moon

could get off scot-free
he remains home in chains
amid the wreckage left behind
by a visit from the Beloved

now look at him, scribbling words
like little paper birds
cutting up shadows into syllables
and, like blowing kisses,
sending them off into the imperfect night

the empty boat

Rumi knows what it's like
to slip like an empty boat
over still water
and be a host to grief
while bravely working

he knows what it's like
to empty the house
for the arrival of the Guest
and make paper chains
for the festivities
even as he plans his exit

he knows how it feels
to bite back tears
and fears
when contemplating the horrendous
state of the world
in its holocaust of madness

he knows that lovers are sleepless
because they feel the secret solitude
of the Beloved all around them

Rumi knows what it's like
to have his words fall flat
just like that
no taking them back
Jack
they're already done
rare, medium, burnt to a crisp

 he knows what it's like
to be a cow that flies
or a goat that barks
or a chicken that never
comes home to roost

all of these things he knows
and other things
too wild to relate
because we'd have to draw
oceans above the sky
and make decent intervals
indecent
until we hardly knew our stops
from our starts

better to leave him in his empty boat
in his boatlessness in his tearlessness
in his wordlessness
in his indecency and his
secret solitude

and be on our way

Extinction Rebellion: a Tribute.
Raising Light Trilogy, 3
(2020)

the intention

I'm in alpine territory
above the tree line
the last clump of birch

I can follow the intention
of the hills, all the way down
to distant green
or back up towards
the promise of snow

moss and rock cling
gravity glides
wind scars the slopes
the sky turns dark honey

there is no horizon
earth and sky just overlap
lips joined in open secrecy

I can lie down here, go soft
on the hard rock
and let the mountain do the dreaming

as we lived

our history will be written in rock

in the fossil records

in broken landscapes

and plastic filled oceans

the planet itself

will be our memorial

and our obituaries will be carved

from violent skies

and a shimmering heat haze

a short-lived species, as species go

for as we lived, we died

soft bandage

when a little gentle rain falls
we make amends

the first shall be last and the last
shall be first
we tell each other

it sounds good that way
a little green springs up
in our mind's eye
a little opening in the heart
to let the truth in
a soft bandage to the wound

we may not have the morrow
but we have the day
we tell ourselves

and the day has just begun

the same world

after the floods, everything grew
fast and rank

then

dried back, died back
and turned to tinder

each morning, we sniff the air
just to make sure
we're in the same world

no longer the sun

no longer those majestic
shafts of light you'll find
in the arched spaces of cathedrals
falling like a blessing
on the land and the people

no longer that zen glimpse
of a hidden garden
suffused with a soft glow
and damp vines of green
and sugary fruit

but rather
a terrible eye that never shuts
that levers open skies
where the light is always hard
and soft things wither away
and stones crack open
in dried river beds

a new sun has been born
pitiless, ferocious
the new god of refugees

stealing flowers

whoever stole flowers

out of time's garden

probably didn't know what they were doing

and ended up with wrinkled hands

failing eyes

and withered blooms

they just saw something bright

and beautiful

and reached out to touch

take

and break

one moment you're wandering along

with barely a care in the world

and a whistle in the air

next thing

you're carrying a bouquet of hours

still fresh

through the market place

where everything's for sale except a carefree

moment

and melodies are quickly forgotten

all those coveted flowers

will fade into the ancient faces of children

and miss their mark

the book

the pages of the text
have blown away
or been tucked in the neck
of Molotov cocktails
soaked in accelerant

the paper was too thin
or
the words too frail
or
the glue came unstuck
or
everything just turned yellow
or
someone got the wrong
end of the stick

the binding was never designed
for the punishment
it is now taking

its pretensions look quite forlorn

and besides, the dead
don't read too good

not as dead

you're never quite as dead
as you think you are

you cut into your flesh
with a razor blade

the relief is instant
you bleed

but the songs of the dead return
with bleak insistence
and there is nothing you can do
nowhere you can go
to make anything feel any better

as long as I draw breath
you say
as you draw another
and another

this is where I died

if you like I can show you
where I died, the exact spot
the moment it came upon me
what I was thinking about
where my hands were placed
and what my feet were doing

even the expected is unexpected
when it happens
right out of the blue

all too soon
the world is at your door

I don't suppose, however
that geography matters much any more
even the dead want to move
to higher ground

I don't suppose the land remembers
beyond a certain point, or has to say

he died there
he was cleaning the car

and listening to the radio
some shock jock
ranting about the evils of immigrants

or she was talking on the cellphone
when worlds collided
and everybody jumped out of their skins

this, then, is where I died
right where you are
right where I said I would be

you can watch it for yourself
in real time
when the moment comes

the houses of sleep

there are eyes that have never belonged
to the sky

faces that can't be found
in trees

feet that have never touched
the earth

bodies that have never known
the love of air

spider minds with no webs

aliens with no memory
of forests

while in the house of sleep
pillows gather dust

Flippity Fluppity Flop:
Nonsense rhymes and Flip
book for the young at heart.
(2021)

One little match-head

little red match-head
sitting on a stick,

watch that match-head
quick! quick! quick!

When it flares brightly
it may burn your hand,

one little red match-head
burns up the land.

Bugle call

I don't want to get up

I don't want to get up

I don't want to get up in the morning.

I'd just as soon stay

in bed all day

cuddled up comfortably snoring.

Poems

At home I have a book of poems

right by my bed,

and every night

one or two poems get read.

Now I've got these poems

floating in my head.

Before

Let me down soft and easy
let me down super slow
let me down sleepways gently
into the satiny snow.

Hold me just for a moment
hold me super slow
hold me while I slip away

before you turn and go.

Run, run, run

Run for the ferry!
Run for the bus!
Run against the clock
make a lot of fuss

That's what my Daddy does
my Mummy does too,
running to the running hands
just to make do.

Sometimes I'm very quiet.
Sometimes I'm toottle-to.
And sometimes I make A GREAT BIG FUSS
'cos I'm running too.

My Mummy

Mummy won't ever listen.
Mummy won't ever hear.

Mummy can't say two-and-six
unless I'm near.

Mummy is a ratbag
Mummy is a geek.
Instead of a nice huggle
there's a peck upon the cheek.

Sometimes Mummy goes away
sometimes she comes back.
Sometimes I'm all alone
and sometimes I'm not.

But when I want my Mummy
there's lots of tears to come
for my Mummy is my Mummy
and I'm her little one.

Sketches

(2022)

labyrinth

looking for you
I find a path I've never walked
through tall trees, manicured lawns
and empty pagodas

like the well-kept grounds
of a private estate

around the path goes
crossing and re-crossing the same stream
the comforting gurgle of water
always near
to the right or left

I didn't find you
but that was alright
far away, you are near
near, you are far away
while the path makes sense to itself
and leads me to this young rimu
green and weeping
among friends

Coromandel wake up

let's wait
allow the water to cool
if it's going to cool

watch Coromandel wake up
to the day's heat haze
or become a dragon
under the reign of shadow

wait for waves to perfect themselves
on the shore

or for the family group
two adults three children
strolling along the water's edge
to grow old

wait for the bees to conclude
their fastidious love affair
with the lupin

and for a host of gulls to gather
out of an abundant past
to pick away at wet sea grass

bird sketches

at dawn, the dotterel is a brief concurrence
of sand and light and wind
the ocean the colour of iced tea

too lazy to use the other
the oyster catcher hops around
on one leg
others bob their heads about
in a curious carousel motion
that may be their rites of spring
performed to the music of their bones

from here
the beach goes on
forever
into the western haze

gulls stand stiff against
falling silver

a piece of driftwood
gets up
and flies away

the power of the eagle

feels easy, lying on our backs
staring up at the clouds
bunched and dark
approaching from the north

the peaks of Rangitoto show
behind the hills of Anzac Bay
blue and grey
with a touch of purple

but nothing is that easy, really
only the words

nearby, a kawakawa wilts
from excessive spray
it's all devastation on the vulnerable
forest floor – the devas have fled
it's too quiet

you finish your sketch
and take out your brush
your water colours trickle into the bay
as the tide comes in

I want to take refuge in the ordinary
but it's not that easy to find
a face forms in the sky but it doesn't hold
long enough to show you

you say, 'if you go to the top of Putiki O Kahu
you will meet the power of the eagle'

it's a long climb

Whakanewha sunrise

It's comic the way the dotterel beetle along
at great speed
the stiff, mechanical movement of their legs
their knees buried in the fluff of their bodies

this is their territory, their hour
their quietitude, their place in the sun
their sky

the sea looks like silk, riding over
a hidden body, faintly ruffled
fragile

there are times I feel so transparent
the world could shine right through me

I remember you dancing at the funeral
your limbs were trying to escape from your torso
your voice had its own body
I didn't have a body, my limbs
were all imaginary

pain is slithering around inside me
looking for a home

that which I once took for granted
now seems miraculous
and that which seemed astonishing
now looks ridiculous

these waves have never known
these shores, and the flesh is still new
to the idea of bones
despite all the time in the world
to get used to it.

I am gathered up in this one place
at least for the moment

we may have been here before
but never right now
and not even then

I deal in homeless lines and feckless rhymes
the door is open, the fish is on the skillet
the debts have been paid

there's always the flax to fall back on
a corner to sleep in
around the curve of the bay

sometimes it comes out just right
sometimes it stays at home
sometimes it has breakfast
sometimes it whips the old gas ring
into flame
and sometimes the sea will rise up
to meet the light

with gestures quick and practiced
you catch
the rough stubble of the peninsula
the boatsheds of Rocky Bay
with all their history
and their new paint jobs

the caspian terns are
a quick sketch in flight
first light fends for itself
among the wiwi

that dead man, he spent a lifetime
walking into the sun
there wasn't much left of him
to bury

could we ever have moved
quiet and unseen
through the world
without leaving a crease?

we ride a fine edge
as the surfer shoots the tube

what is this, our little country
but a brief pause between eruptions.

Putiki Point

(On hearing Leila Lees read her poem,
Ferry Crossing)

ferry glimpses of the past
one wave at a time
one pencil line
after another
light, faint and nerveless

when the sun appears
white caps turn silver
while the voices of our ancestors
recede
like an island fading to a speck

in your voice I hear
the generations of women
the westerlies they face
in their homes under the sea
the dip, glide and shudder
of their flesh
the forgetfulness of history

I see those women in their lonely

settler lives, their sky windows

their rough beds

the shadows in the corner of their eyes

their wandering deaths

and when you finish reading

your voice folds under the wake

bright and pearly in water colours

beach walk

it wasn't like that
the way it sounds

nothing out of the ordinary happened

my hat stayed on my head
you kept your counsel
and no one else came by

even the dog walkers stayed away

there was a pile of burnt sticks
where someone had made a fire

detritus along the grass line
from the last storm surge

a wet, bare expanse
left by the ebbing tide

I took off my shoes and numbed my feet

in the waves

nobody was swimming

I thought I heard someone speak

but when I turned around

I was the only one there

you were far off, by the rocks

lifting the sky into place

with a piece of charcoal

movement

the old path's been washed away
and leads to
a tangle of pōhutukawa roots

the rising sea has sculptured
caves of clay
where gnarly creatures live

here comes the sun
on the back of a seagull's wing

voices from all over
echo across the water
the sad tale of humankind

the death of things makes for
a special quiet
thought overlies it all

it was never meant to be definitive
never meant to show more
than a face

we sit on the damp sand
not caring about the cold
seeping up through our history

the terns sit quietly
like flecks of light
riding the wave

you could make a Ming vase
out of the sky
the shape I mean
the long curve of a life lived
to reach this point

your cellphone lies on the sand
its black face blank
we can't be reached
but for those tangled roots
deep in fantasy

who can we count upon
we keep asking

goodbye Fyodor, goodbye Virginia
Dante has a special heaven sorted for us
where ancient harmonies rule

and the envelope of consciousness
is as fragrant as lavender

the gull turns down my invitation to dance
but that's alright
I didn't mean it anyway

I'm happy enough waiting
for the trees to release the sky
cloud stripped
and send us all reeling

the ruru doesn't cry much
beyond the dawn

it's all about movement, you say
the pen makes its mark
and there's no rubbing it out

Palm Beach in the age of Covid 19

a white dog with yellow eyes

comes visiting

indifferent to social distancing

wants to lick something

we put our bodies into the ocean

and give over our frail weight

to its buoyancy

our feet bob up

an ocean away from our heads

in our isolation

we each discover ourselves

get to meet who we are

after the supermarket shelves

go empty

the dog tells me that eternity

is not forever

eternity is endlessness

the forever beach
on the forever sand
is no more than
the endlessness of the
moving moment
forged in the flare of stars

we are but a song
stretched over bone
held together
by sinews of light

a lone swimmer strokes the waves
my words leave no trace on the page

the dog happily returns to the
lolloping world
fancying her chances

fingers laced, we stay
where we are
and wait it out

Thompson's Point

If, in the future, someone
tries to find this old wooden gate
with a view over grassy hills
I doubt they'll have much luck

that gate has the look of something
that won't last, that's already history

which opens from a farm track
which has turned into a road
into a farm which has turned into a
real estate development

the borderlines are marked
the earth movers have arrived
the first turf turned

like me, the gate is having a problem
with one of its hinges
we can just grow together
old, decrepit and unhinged
until big shiny things
take our place

From the slopes of Ruapehu

1
dawn discovers the mountain
in the palest pastels

they say there's trouble brewing in the crater
all looks sweet to me
but for a certain ponderous silence

the chaffinch, light and airy
is still around
to flirt with the light

along the mountain streams, the sleek stoat
still hunts for fresh-water cray

the kestrel still chases the quick-witted wax eyes
between the shadows

a little rain still quickens rock pools

a wispy trace of cloud
vanishes in the moment

2

this point marks the furthest advance of the lava flow
this Tolkienesque bunch of rocks is as far
as the magma could reach

here, it's all about shape and density

high up
with a deep valley either side

feels like a good place, I say
to witness an eruption

3

light can't be stopped
everything it touches, it frees

in a moment or two it will touch
this bench on which I'm sitting
and free me

4

I'm too close to death
to feel entirely comfortable

5

if I have to die
let it be with the sound of water
running through my head

all the wind would need to do
is close my eyes

6

since I'm in no hurry to get to where I'm going
it takes no time at all

we pause to discuss the colour of the tiny flowers
of the heather
are they white or touched with pink
is there mauve in there somewhere
or can they just recall
as a fragile memory
the russet red of leaves

7

it becomes all about light
   unalloyed light
   uncompromised light
   spacious light
in the uncluttered air

passing through

tūī arrives to drink from the spouting

blackbird flies in through the open window

and scratches around on the kitchen bench

pīwakawaka flicks sideways

from glance to glance

thrush gives throat to the world

kereru performs an elegant dive

from blue to green

the end of the day may fall into place

with a basketful of ripe plums

half-pecked

and some regrets

the armies of night

return home, their helmets blazing

a snarl of traffic at the roundabout

the soft-winged ruru flies by night

an old moon lies in the arms of the young

a trick of the eye

outside my window

there's a tūī

sliding

with quick, deft movements

between the pink branches

of the spring plum

with a touch of white blossom at its throat

at Auckland Hospital

we are at the bottom
of a well of light

in a place with no shadows

we chat to keep away the silence
the dead walk on slippers

there are a lot of gaps to fill
or jump across

all the words are made of the same
structural grey steel

follow the yellow line

of this human suffering
no voice can tell
and perhaps there is some wonder here
after all

a miracle being wheeled somewhere
on a trolley bed

there's always somebody worse off
somebody says

coffee machine goes whoosh-sizzle

at Found - Surfdale

the waitress writes our order

on the back of her hand

the fleshy part

gospel music

plays softly

while hot tea warms the soul

at the table, we have

a petunia moment

between words

I return to the beginning

but don't find myself there

a white dog wanders between the tables

winter rain

when a gentle rain falls
we make amends

you were the first
and you will be the last
we tell each other
over tea and toast
as the dark lifts
and lovers line up for their kisses

it sounds good that way
a little green springs up
in our mind's eye
a little jump in the heart
at a touch
a soft bandage to the wound
the scent of creamy sandalwood
sweet horsetail
and sexy patchouli

the sky licks the earth

with a slushy tongue

the pond refills, and we wonder

if the slidey eel will return

tūī rejoice in the guttering

pīwakawaka come out to play

humans hold their heartbeat

in their hands

far off, a world sings

of love

and all that has been forgotten

we may not have the morrow

but we have the day

we tell ourselves

and the day has just begun

Poetry Bibliography

The Palanquin Ropes. Wellington: Voice Press, 1983.
From a Woman in Mt Eden Prison & Drawing Lessons. Auckland: Hard Echo Press, 1984.

Standing Wave. Auckland: Hard Echo Press, 1985.

'The Children are Singing.' *Span 23* (September 1986). Ed. Peter Simpson & Simon Garrett (Christchurch: South Pacific Association for Commonwealth Literature and Language Studies, 1986), pp.48-55.

Treasure Hunt. Auckland: Auckland University Press, 1996.

The Vertical Harp: Selected Poems of Li He. Auckland: Titus Books, 2006.

To Beatrice Where We Cross The Line. Auckland: Sandwich Press, 2014.

Two Lines And A Garden. Drawings by Leila Lees. 99% Press. Waiheke, Auckland: Lasavia Publishing Ltd., 2017.

Ladder With No Rungs. Prints by Leila Lees. 99% Press. Waiheke, Auckland: Lasavia Publishing Ltd., 2019.

The Toy Box. Raising Light Trilogy, 1. 99% Press. Waiheke, Auckland: Lasavia Publishing Ltd., 2020.

Hide Your Eyes: The Rumi Poems. Raising Light Trilogy, 2. 99% Press. Waiheke, Auckland: Lasavia Publishing Ltd., 2020.

Extinction Rebellion: A Tribute. Raising Light Trilogy, 3. 99% Press. Waiheke, Auckland: Lasavia Publishing Ltd., 2020.

[with Daniela Gast]. *Flippity Fluppity Flop: Nonsense rhymes and Flip book for the young at heart*. Bean Sprout Press. Waiheke, Auckland: Lasavia Publishing Ltd., 2021.

Sketches. Drawings by Leila Lees. 99% Press. Waiheke, Auckland: Lasavia Publishing Ltd., 2022.

Jack Ross has edited numerous collections of writing and a variety of journals. Ross has worked as a teacher of New Zealand literature and creative writing, and he is co-editor of a series of books dedicated to capturing New Zealand poets in performance. He was also editor of Poetry New Zealand for five years.

Mike Johnson, fiction writer and poet, is widely regarded as one of New Zealand's most innovative writers. He lives on Waiheke Island and has taught creative writing at AUT University and the University of Auckland. In 2002 he received The University of Auckland's Literary Fellowship, having been Literary Fellow at Canterbury University in 1987. His first novel, *Lear, the Shakespeare Company Plays Lear at Babylon* was short listed for the New Zealand Book Awards in 1986, his novel *Dumb Show* won the Buckland Memorial Award for Literary Excellence in 1995, and he won the Frances Kean Award his short story, 'Magic Strings' in 1999. His first book of poetry, *The Palanquin Ropes*, (1983) was co-winner of the John Cowie Reed Memorial Competition. His non-fiction, *Angel of Compassion*, was shortlisted for the Ashton Whyle Award in 2014, and a poem from *Vertical Harp, The selected poems of Li He* (2006) has been anthologised in the *Essential New Zealand Poems: Facing the Empty Page* (Random House, 2015). Mike Johnson is the author of twenty-six books including nine books of poetry, three of shorter fiction, one non fiction, three children's books, and ten novels.

Also by Mike Johnson

Novels
Stench
Driftdead
Lethal Dose
Zombie in a Spacesuit
Hold My Teeth While I Teach You to Dance
Travesty
Counterpart
Dumbshow
Antibody Positive
Lear: The Shakespeare Company Plays Lear at Babylon

Shorter Fiction
Confessions of a Cockroach/Headstone
Back in the Day: Tales of NZ's Own Paradise Island
Foreigners

Poetry
Sketches
The Raising Light Trilogy
Ladder With No Rungs, Illustrated by Leila Lees
Two Lines and a Garden, Illustrated by Leila Lees
To Beatrice: Where We Crossed the Line
Vertical Harp: The Selected Poems of Li He
Treasure Hunt
Standing Wave
From a Woman in Mt Eden Prison & Drawing Lessons
The Palanquin Ropes

Non-Fiction
Angel of Compassion

Children's Books
Flippity Fluppity Flop, Illustrated by Daniela Gast
A House With No Windows, Illustrated by Ingrid Berzins
Kenni and the Roof Slide, Illustrated by Jennifer Rackham
Taniwha. Illustrated by Jennifer Rackham

www.ingramcontent.com/pod-product-compliance
Lightning Source LLC
Chambersburg PA
CBHW031510120626
46545CB00005B/1826